MW00614415

Goodwill
Toward Men

An Introduction to

The War Is Over

Andrew Wommack

© Copyright 2023 – Andrew Wommack

Printed in the United States of America. All rights reserved. No portion of this book may be reproduced, stored in a retrieval system, or transmitted in any form or by any means—electronic, mechanical, photocopy, recording, scanning, or other—except for brief quotations in critical reviews or articles, without the prior written permission of the publisher.

Unless otherwise indicated, all Scripture quotations are taken from the King James Version® of the Bible. Copyright © by the British Crown. Public domain.

All emphasis within Scripture quotations is the author's own.

Published in partnership between Andrew Wommack Ministries and Harrison House Publishers.

Woodland Park, CO 80863 – Shippensburg, PA 17257

ISBN 13 TP: 978-1-59548-582-3

For Worldwide Distribution, Printed in the USA

2 3 4 5 6 / 26 25 24 23

Introduction

And [Mary] brought forth her firstborn son, and wrapped him in swaddling clothes, and laid him in a manger; because there was no room for them in the inn. And there were in the same country shepherds abiding in the field, keeping watch over their flock by night. And, lo, the angel of the Lord came upon them, and the glory of the Lord shone round about them: and they were sore afraid.

And the angel said unto them, Fear not: for, behold, I bring you good tidings of great joy, which shall be to all people. For unto you is born this day in the city of David a Saviour, which is Christ the Lord. And this shall be a sign unto you; Ye shall find the babe wrapped in swaddling clothes, lying in a manger. And suddenly there was with the angel a multitude of the heavenly host praising God, and saying, Glory to God in the highest, and on earth peace, good will toward men.

Luke 2:7–14

Overcoming Religious Tradition

Luke 2:7–14 is a familiar passage of scripture recounting the birth of Jesus. All too often, we use it to create a certain mood and get ourselves into the "Christmas spirit." The problem is, we don't really think about what it is actually saying, or even worse, we've interpreted this in the wrong way.

In verse 14, the heavenly host declares, *"Glory to God in the highest, and on earth peace, good will toward men."*

Most people interpret this as the angels proclaiming peace among men, but that is definitely not what they were rejoicing about. This was speaking of peace from God towards men. They were celebrating the end of the war between God and man through the sacrifice of Jesus and all that would bring.

Jesus, Himself made it clear that He didn't come to bring peace among men. Jesus said in Matthew 10:34–36:

Think not that I am come to send peace on earth: I came not to send peace, but a sword. For I am come to set a man at variance against his father, and the daughter against her mother, and the daughter in law against her mother in law. And a man's foes shall be *they of his own household.*

Jesus said He did not come to give peace on earth among men. As a matter of fact, the Lord also prophesied that one of the signs of the end times would be increased war, division, and strife. In Matthew 24:6–8, He said:

And ye shall hear of wars and rumours of wars: see that ye be not troubled: for all these things *must come to pass, but the end is not yet. For nation shall rise against nation, and kingdom against kingdom . . . . All these* are *the beginning of sorrows.*

You may be familiar with the Christmas carol that goes, "I heard the bells on Christmas day their old, familiar carols play; and wild and sweet the words repeat of peace on earth, good will to men." It's based on the poem "Christmas Bells" written by Henry Wadsworth Longfellow in the 1860s after his son was severely wounded in the Civil War. One of the song's verses says, "'There is no peace on earth,' I said, 'for hate is strong, and mocks the song of peace on earth, good will to men.'" Because of the war, Longfellow was doubting the angels' proclamation in Luke 2:14.

I believe there is a common misunderstanding of what it means to have peace on earth. In Matthew 5:9, Jesus said, *"Blessed* are *the peacemakers: for they shall be called the children of God."* Notice this does not say, "blessed are the peace*keepers.*" What is a peacemaker? It is not a pacifist. A pacifist always rejects war or fighting as a way of settling disputes. But a peacemaker is a person who seeks and promotes peace.

Sometimes, the best way to promote peace is to fight and put yourself in harm's way. British Prime Minister Neville Chamberlain was a pacifist who thought he could prevent war by making deals with Adolf Hitler in the late 1930s and preserve "peace for our time." But as Winston Churchill said of World War II, "There never was a war in history easier to prevent by timely action."[1] If someone had stood up to Hitler before he invaded neighboring countries and seized their assets, he could have been easily stopped. The Allies fought for peace in World War II. They were peacemakers. Jesus was a peacemaker between God and mankind.

Peace on Earth

Jesus actually distinguished God's peace from what the world calls peace. In John 14:27, He said:

Peace I leave with you, my peace I give unto you: not as the world giveth, give I unto you. Let not your heart be troubled, neither let it be afraid.

In the world's mentality, peace is the absence of conflict. Just as Longfellow wrote, many people believe that if there is war between men, there is no peace on earth. However, God's peace is not dependent on circumstances. When the angels were singing, *"glory*

> **Jesus was a peacemaker between God and mankind.**

to God in the highest, and on earth peace, good will toward men" (Luke 2:14), they were talking about peace from God *toward* men, not peace among men.

I will grant that if a person receives the Gospel and gets their heart changed, they will treat people differently. I'm sure that there are millions of examples of people who have walked in peace and their lives have been changed; but this verse isn't prophesying or speaking about peace among men. It is talking about peace from God *to* man.

When I served in Vietnam, there certainly wasn't peace among men. Our fire support base was maybe 100 feet by 200 feet large, and we took hundreds of mortar rounds in that small area. Eventually the base was overrun by the Viet Cong, and we had to evacuate; but I was rejoicing because I thought, *Jesus, I might be with You before the end of the day*. I even prayed for those Vietnamese fighters who were coming up that hill trying to kill me. It was like I was in a bubble because I had the peace of God.

There didn't seem to be peace in the middle of the Civil War either; but later on in his poem, Wadsworth ended up writing, "Then pealed the bells more loud and deep: 'God is not dead, nor doth He sleep; the wrong shall fail, the right prevail, with peace on earth, good will to men.'" Jesus didn't come to keep peace among men; He came to make peace between God and man.

How God Dealt with Sin

To fully appreciate what I'm saying, you have to understand that under the Old Covenant, there was war—God declared war on sin.

Some people don't understand this, and they look at things that happened in the Old Testament, thinking God was too harsh. Some people have this impression of God being angry and bitter—that He is just waiting for you to get out of line so He can smite you.

When we look at how God dealt with sin in the Old Testament, it relates to how parents discipline their children when they are little. A parent can't just tell a one- or two-year-old, "Don't do that because you're giving place to the devil, and the devil only comes to steal, kill, and destroy (John 10:10); he's going to make you sick, he's going to ruin your marriage, you'll never keep a job," and on and on. You can't reason with that child, but you can tell them, "If you do that again, you're going to get a spanking." They may not even understand that there is a God or a devil, heaven or hell, or any of those other things; but before they think about doing that same wrong thing again, they will associate it with pain.

When our oldest son was just about two years old, we were walking out in the country on a dirt road. The weeds were up around four or five feet high. He was just a tiny little boy, running up about thirty yards ahead of us. We were walking and talking because nobody ever came down this dirt road. But there was an intersection up ahead, and a car was coming down that dirt road at fifty to sixty miles per hour. The car was coming so fast that I couldn't have run quickly enough to physically stop my son.

Joshua reached the intersection at the exact moment the car was whizzing by. The weeds were high, and the driver couldn't see him. They were on a collision course. But we had been training him to obey us. If he didn't, he got a spanking. So, I shouted, "Joshua, stop!" He froze midstride while that car zoomed on by, just a few feet away.

Many people don't discipline their kids. They just think they ought to reason with them, but young children don't have the mental capacity to understand at that point. In a similar way, before someone is born again, they just don't have the capacity to understand spiritual things. So then, how could God restrict the amount of sin being committed? How could He get us pointed in the right direction and doing the right thing, even though we didn't have the capacity for spiritual understanding before being born again? God had to create the law to teach people right and wrong. He made fear of consequences their motivation for obedience.

Mercy vs. Judgment

Romans 5:13 is a pivotal scripture that's helped me understand the entire Bible:

For until the law sin was in the world: but sin is not imputed when there is no law.

It says, *"until the law."* That's during the time of Moses. The law was given nearly 2,500 years after the fall of Adam. Until then, God wasn't imputing men's sins unto them.

The word *impute* means "to hold against." It's actually an accounting term. If you bought something and said, "Put that on my account," they would write it down. Then, at the end of the month, you'd have to pay up. Until the time that the law was given, man sinned; but God wasn't holding their sins against them. This is a major piece of information!

Basically, our whole religious system has taught us that God is this holy, stern, austere God who's angry and cannot tolerate sinners. For many people, this is their impression of God. Religion has taught us that when Adam and Eve sinned (Gen. 3:1–7), God instantly cast them out of His presence because He couldn't stand to put up with sinful man. We're told that the wrath of God was instantly vented upon the earth.

But God was still walking and talking with mankind. God sent Adam and Eve *out* of the Garden of Eden so they wouldn't take of the tree of life, and eat, and live forever in a fallen state (Gen. 3:22–23). It would have been terrible to live forever in a sinful state. Because we live in a sinful world, death can actually

Our whole religious system has taught us that God is...angry and cannot tolerate sinners.

be a good thing. Now, I can just hear books closing everywhere because of that last statement, but think about it for a moment. If people couldn't die, then all of the Hitlers, Stalins, Pol Pots, and Idi Amins of the world would still be alive and spewing their poison. Death puts an end to a lot of things.

What would it be like to live in a fallen world, but not be able to die? You'd live life forever in this corrupted, sinful state. You would live forever in a place where there's lying, cheating, stealing, and every conceivable evil practice going on everywhere all the time. In light of this, death really is a benefit. Until the time of Moses, God wasn't holding men's sins against them. God was and still is a merciful God. He didn't instantly start judging man and bringing punishment upon his sin. God was actually operating in mercy toward men for nearly the first 2,500 years of existence. Then the law came.

God has always wanted to relate to us by grace, but He couldn't just look the other way and ignore sin. The sin debt had to be paid.

Under the Old Covenant

Under the Old Covenant, people couldn't be born again. If a person ever gave place to the devil, they could become demon-possessed through idol worship, bestiality, homosexuality, and even being rebellious toward parents. Once people crossed that line and just gave themselves over to the devil, God dealt with sin like a cancer or an infection. Just as a doctor would have to cut off the infected part to preserve the body, God was severe with wrath.

I remember a man coming to a meeting seeking prayer, and he was holding a towel over his face. He was talking to me, but I couldn't really hear him. So, I said, "I'm sorry, but I cannot understand you. You are going to have to remove that towel to talk to me."

When he removed the towel, I could see that cancer had eaten away his nose and other parts of his face and mouth. It was just grotesque looking. He had fluids that were pouring out, which is part of the reason he was using a towel. At that same set of meetings, I saw another man who lost an eye to cancer, and it spread over the left side of his face until his whole head was deformed.

Those are terrible things, but that's how cancer works. It's also how sin works on a person or a nation, which is why God had to cut those things off so they would not spread through His people. Because people couldn't be born again and couldn't be delivered from those things, it was actually an act of mercy on God's part to purge that ungodliness out of the human race.

It's like in Exodus 32, when the children of Israel sacrificed before the golden calf and engaged in all manner of wantonness including fornication and adultery (v. 6, *"rose up to play"*) while Moses was receiving the Ten Commandments on Mt. Sinai. Not only were they engaging in idolatry, but they were also corrupting themselves with all kinds of debauchery!

In Exodus 32:10, God said to Moses, *"...let me alone, that my wrath may wax hot against them, and that I may consume them."*

God had every right to be angry with the Israelites. They had seen the demonstration of His glory as no people had ever seen before, yet in just a matter of days, they had turned from the true and living God to worship idols. They deserved whatever punishment the Lord saw fit to give them.

Even though Moses interceded on the people's behalf (Exod. 32:11–13) so God wouldn't wipe out all of them, something had to be done. The Bible says about three thousand men died by the sword that same day (Exod. 32:28). This may seem like harsh judgment, but it was justified. These people were totally rebellious toward the Lord. In those days, before a person could be born again and become a totally new creature in Christ (2 Cor. 5:17), evil had to be rooted out, or it would infect the whole nation.

But now, because of Jesus, God deals with mankind differently. And in the same way, we aren't supposed to be serving God out of fear of punishment.

Under the New Covenant

In Acts 13:39, the apostle Paul said of the New Covenant made in Jesus' blood: "...*all that believe are justified from all things, from which ye could not be justified by the law of Moses.*"

Justification is the act of God that makes us totally righteous in His sight. To accomplish this, the Lord not only forgives our sins but also imparts His righteousness. This makes you and me justified or "just-as-if-I'd" never sinned. Under the Old Testament law, many things were unpardonable and carried the death sentence. But through Jesus, we can now receive forgiveness from these things and enjoy right standing with God.

> **We aren't supposed to be serving God out of fear of punishment.**

It's like if you had an infection, the options are cut off a part of your hand so that the infection doesn't spread or take antibiotics to kill the infection and save the hand. God no longer cuts people off like a cancer when they sin. That was only a temporary way God dealt with us until we could be born again.

Now that we're new creatures in Christ (2 Cor. 5:17), we have an intuitive knowledge. God is inside us, informing us of right and wrong, and leading us in the way we should go. As a Christian, you don't have to fear the wrath and judgment of God. Most people haven't understood this. They're still operating under Old Covenant fear. They're afraid that God is angry with them and that He's imputing sin unto them. This needs to change.

I grew up near a busy city street. My mother would spank me if I ever crossed that street without looking both ways. I received many spankings over that.

So here I am, decades later as a mature adult, and I still look both ways two or three times whenever I cross a street. "Look

> As a Christian, you don't have to fear the wrath and judgment of God.

both ways before you cross the street," was literally beaten into me. Now I understand that it's not about avoiding punishment. I've gone way beyond that. I do what's right, not because I'll get in trouble, but because I don't want to be hit by a car.

My mother has gone on to be with the Lord, and I don't have to be afraid of her spanking me anymore. Now I do what's right but from a totally different motivation. Likewise, I don't fear the Law anymore, but I still live holy because it's the best way to live.

The Word Became Flesh

What God did by sending Jesus to be born is something we should rejoice about all year long—not just at Christmastime. Now, I enjoy Christmas, but it is about more than just a season or an emotional feeling.

When we read Luke 2:10–11, we learn about the greatest miracle of all time: God became flesh:

And the angel said unto them, Fear not: for, behold, I bring you good tidings of great joy, which shall be to all people. For unto you is born this day in the city of David a Saviour, which is Christ the Lord.

Jesus was the Lord at His birth. He didn't grow into becoming God. Jesus' physical body grew, and He had to renew His mind. Luke 2:52 says, *"Jesus increased in wisdom and in stature, and in favour with God and man,"* but He was God almighty at birth. The word, *Lord* in verse 11 is the exact same word that is used to refer to the Lord God hundreds of times in the New Testament. So, Jesus was God at birth, placed in a human body as a baby.

After all these years, I still can't totally comprehend it.

You see, the Scripture says the entire universe fits in the span of God's hand (Is. 40:12). That's talking about the width of His hand, from the tip of His thumb to the tip of His little finger. God's hand is wider than the entire universe. According to what scientists say, the universe is hundreds of billions of light years wide; and it all fits in God's hand. And to think, the creator of the universe, who could fit it all in His hand, came to earth as a baby to become like one of us. That's awesome!

It was a man—a physical human being—who had been given authority on the earth by God (Gen. 1:26–28). When man allowed himself to be deceived and yielded his power to Satan (Gen. 3:1–19), he became, in a sense, joint-heirs with the devil. Satan has to work through a human being. Man, through his physical body, gave Satan authority on this earth. Therefore, it was necessary for a man with a physical body to take back that authority. God had to become man (Jesus), to give Him the authority to execute judgment on the earth (John 5:27). God cannot break or change His word, so He was restricted to act within the word He had already spoken.

Jesus Lifted Up

God could not just come down here and solve all the problems of the earth because it says in John 4:24

that God is a spirit. He gave authority over the earth to people with physical human bodies, so this is why Jesus had to become a man. He also had to have a physical body so He could have authority to defeat the devil and bring back the people that God loved. This is what the angels were celebrating!

God was born in human form, and the wrath of God for people's sin was going to be placed upon Jesus. The wrath that God had been exhibiting toward the human race in the Old Covenant was going to be done away with. God's love was going to be released.

In John 12, Jesus had just heard an audible voice from His father saying, *"I have both glorified [My Name], and will glorify it again,"* and the people heard it. Some of them thought it was thunder while others thought it was an angel speaking to Him (vv. 28–29).

Jesus said in verses 30–32, *"This voice came not because of me, but for your sakes. Now is the judgment of this world: now shall the prince of this world be cast out. And I, if I be lifted up from the earth, will draw all* **men** *unto me."*

Most people interpret this to mean that if we just lift up Jesus through preaching and glorify Him properly, He'll draw everyone to Himself. But that's not what it's talking about. The word *men* in the *King James Version* is italicized. This is one of the reasons I like this version of the Bible because the translators were at least honest enough to tell you if they inserted a word that wasn't there in the original language. You can't always just translate things directly.

So, the word *men* here in verse 32 is italicized. What that means is Jesus literally said, *"And I, if I be lifted up from the earth, will draw all unto me."* The translators just made it "all *men*," but if you read it in context, you'll see something. The previous verse says, *"Now is the judgment of this world...."* And the next verse, right after it, says, *"I . . . will draw all unto me."* Verse 33 says, *"This he said, signifying what death he should die."*

Jesus wasn't talking about just lifting Him up through honoring and proclaiming Him properly.

He was talking about when He would get lifted up on the cross and crucified, He would draw all of God's *judgment* unto Him. Did you know God punished Jesus for what we did? All of God's wrath against your sin and my sin—everything that you and I have ever done wrong—was put on Jesus.

God Is Just

The Bible says, *"The soul that sinneth, it shall die"* (Ezek. 18:20), and *"the wages of sin is death"* (Rom. 6:23). God is just. He couldn't just say, "Well, I love you, so I'm going to let you go, even though you've sinned and deserve judgment." No! God had to judge our sin, but He didn't want to judge us. There's none of us that deserve the goodness of God. Romans 3:23 says, *"all have sinned, and come short of the glory of God."* So, how could a just God have relationship with us if we are defiled?

> All of God's wrath against your sin and my sin...was put on Jesus.

Isaiah 59:1–2 says:

Behold, the LORD's hand is not shortened, that it cannot save; neither his ear heavy, that it cannot hear: but your iniquities have separated between you and your God, and your sins have hid his face from you, that he will not hear.

God's wrath came upon us because He's just, and sin has to be judged. But when Jesus came, He took all of God's judgment for our sin into His own body so that God could say, "Your sins are paid for." Instead of making us pay for sin, His Son came to this earth and paid for sin for us. This is what the angels were rejoicing about when they sang, *"Glory to God in the highest, and on earth peace, good will toward men"* (Luke 2:14).

God can release peace toward you and me, even though we've all sinned and don't deserve it. If we got what we deserved, every last one of us would go to hell. There's nobody that deserves God's goodness. But people compare themselves among themselves. This is a huge mistake. That's what the Scripture says over in 2 Corinthians 10:12:

For we dare not make ourselves of the number, or compare ourselves with some that commend themselves: but they measuring themselves by themselves, and comparing themselves among themselves, are not wise.

This is what people seem to do all the time. They think, *Well I'm a relatively good person and so I know that God's going to accept me.* No! God doesn't accept you based on what you do. It's not as if your good deeds outweigh your bad and that's what gets you into heaven. It's not that good people go to heaven and bad people go to hell. Good people don't go to heaven. It's forgiven people that go to heaven!

> God can release peace toward you and me, even though we've all sinned and don't deserve it.

Jesus Became Sin

Nobody deserves to go to heaven. You have to be forgiven. And the only reason we can be forgiven is because the Word (Jesus) became flesh and took our sin into His own body and received all of God's judgment.

That's what Jesus was talking about when He said, *"If I be lifted up from the earth"* (John 12:32). All of God's judgment was drawn to Him on the cross.

This is why Jesus said, "Eloi, Eloi, lama sabachthani?" ("My God, my God, why hast thou forsaken me?") in Mark 15:34. That's a quotation from Psalm 22:1.

In verses 3 and 4 of that same Psalm, we find out why God forsook Him:

> *But thou art holy, O thou that inhabitest the praises of Israel. Our fathers trusted in thee: they trusted, and thou didst deliver them.*

The reason God forsook Jesus is because Jesus had to become sin for us. Second Corinthians 5:21 says:

For [God] hath made him to be sin for us, who knew no sin; that we might be made the righteousness of God in him.

Jesus didn't just take a little bit of punishment. He took the entire wrath of God against us into His *"own body on the tree, that we, being dead to sins, should live unto righteousness..."* (1 Pet. 2:24).

This is why the angels were singing *"Glory to God in the highest, and on earth peace"* (Luke 2:14) from God toward man. God could now be merciful to you and me, not because we deserved it—not because we've done everything right—but because Jesus bore our sin! If you understand that, it just changes everything! It would take away any arrogance on your part about your perceived goodness. I don't know how anybody can have a revelation of Jesus bearing their sins, dying, going to hell for them, and suffering for three days, and then feel proud about who they are. I'm not

> **The reason God forsook Jesus is because Jesus had to become sin for us.**

denying that God has blessed me and used me, but it's all because of what Jesus did. It is not because of anything I did. Psalm 39:5 says, *"...every man at his best state* is *altogether vanity."*

I guarantee you, if you could understand that the angels were glorifying God because there was finally a way to bring reconciliation with mankind by having Jesus take our punishment, it would change the way you see things. And you would be doing everything you could to tell others about it!

Reconciling the World

Second Corinthians 5:19 says, *"God was in Christ, reconciling the world unto himself, not imputing their trespasses unto them; and hath committed unto us the word of reconciliation."*

Notice the phrase *"God was in Christ . . . not imputing."* "Not imputing" would be like using a credit card to purchase something, yet it is never charged to your bill. That amount isn't held against you. This verse says that "God was in Christ," not holding man's sins against them.

Contrary to popular opinion, people don't go to hell because of their sins.

And [Jesus] is the propitiation for our sins: and not for ours only, but also for the sins of the whole world.

1 John 2:2

They go to hell because they rejected the payment for their sins. They go to hell because they refused to receive the Savior. Sin is no longer the issue. Now, it's a matter of what people are doing with Jesus. Have they made a commitment of their life to Him, or are they rejecting Him? If someone doesn't receive Jesus as their Savior, they reject the only payment available for their sins. There's no other way to the Father except through His Son (John 14:6).

So, if they don't accept the payment for their sins—the Lord Jesus Christ—they'll be rejected and cast into hell, not because of their sins, but because of rejecting Jesus. In hell, they'll be held accountable and have to pay for those sins. But the truth is, all of those sins have already been paid for by Jesus. This is the word that the church should be preaching.

God's not angry. He's not even in a bad mood. He loves you and has paid the price for you. We are supposed to be having the same ministry Jesus had—and God, in Christ, did not impute man's sins unto them. He reconciled the world unto Himself. Second Corinthians 5:20 says, *"Now then we are ambassadors for Christ."* In a sense, that's what the ministry of reconciliation is like: we are representing God's Kingdom among those who are *"strangers from the covenants of promise"* (Eph. 2:12).

Ambassadors don't just go over to other nations and proclaim whatever they want. They must be faithful to their home country so they can accurately represent it. For instance, every United States ambassador represents the president

> **God's not angry. He's not even in a bad mood.**

and the people of the United States of America. They aren't free to make up their own message. Their job is to accurately represent those who have sent them. As believers, we are supposed to be doing the same thing. We're supposed to be representing God accurately.

Sin Is No Longer an Issue

Jesus—both by His life and His message— declared, "God isn't mad at you anymore. Your sins aren't a problem!"

If you have already received the Lord Jesus Christ, then you've been born again. God isn't angry with you over your sin. The Lord wants you to stop focusing on sin and start receiving His love. Many Christians would like to stone you for standing up and saying, "Your sin isn't a problem with God." They'll ask, "How could you say such a thing? You're making light of sin. You're acting as though there is nothing wrong with sin."

No, that's not what I'm saying. I'm not encouraging anyone to sin.

Anyone who takes what I'm sharing and says, "This is awesome. I love it! Now I can go live in sin," needs to be born again. (If you haven't accepted Jesus Christ as your Lord and Savior, there's a prayer you can pray at the end of this booklet.)

First John 3:3 says, *"Every man that hath this hope in him purifieth himself, even as he is pure."* If you are truly born again and have the hope of being like Jesus, then you're looking for a way to overcome sin—not indulge it.

If you take what I'm saying and tell people, "Andrew is encouraging people to sin," you're either lying or you've misunderstood what I'm communicating. When people accuse me of making light of sin, I respond, "You're making light of Jesus!" I'm not saying that sin isn't bad and that you can just go live in it. Sin is terrible, but it's not as big as Jesus.

The Lord paid for our sins (1 Cor. 6:20). The payment He made is infinitely greater than the sins of the entire world. One drop of Jesus' blood was more holy, more righteous, and more pure than all of the impurity and ungodliness of this entire world put together. If somehow you could find a set of scales large enough and put all the sins of the entire world on one side and the sacrifice of Jesus on

Sin is terrible, but it's not as big as Jesus.

the other, it might just topple over. It's like God put His hand on the scale. There's just no comparison!

If you were to approach God through the atonement of Jesus, you would be able to enter *"boldly unto the throne of grace, that [you] may obtain mercy, and find grace to help in time of need"* (Heb. 4:16), not because you have done everything right, but because Jesus paid such a price that you could have confidence to enter into the presence of God. He's not mad at you anymore—the war is over!

When the Lord Jesus Christ died for our sins, His sacrifice forever satisfied the wrath of God.

Jesus Paid It All

Even though there are many people reading this booklet who are born again, I would say most of the people I minister to do not really have an understanding of what I am teaching. When the average believer messes up, they somehow or another feel that they've got to do penance or suffer for a period of time until it equals the sin that they've committed. That is what's called "double jeopardy." That's a person thinking, *Jesus didn't pay enough, so I've also got to suffer.* That's just wrong!

It isn't honoring to God for me to go around saying, "I'm just an old sinner saved by grace." No! I *was* an "old sinner," but I've been saved by grace. I have now been made *"the righteousness of God in [Christ]"* (2 Cor. 5:21). It is humility for me to just say, "Father, I don't deserve it in myself, but I receive it."

Jesus paid for it. He paid more than I had to pay and because of it, I can enter *"boldly unto the throne of grace"* (Heb. 4:16). It honors God to do that. But to go around thinking, *Jesus, I know you suffered, but*

I've also got to suffer because I'm so unworthy and I've done so many wrong things, doesn't honor God.

If you could imagine that I was God, and if I loved you so much that I literally took one of my sons and I sacrificed him—put all of my wrath, all of my punishment, all of my hatred for your sins upon my son—and saw him crucified him and die so that I could accept you, I wouldn't have done it if it didn't pay the price completely.

Jesus suffered. He bore our punishment from God, His Father. Isaiah 52:14 says, *"His visage was so marred more than any man, and his form more than the sons of men."* The word *visage* is a word that we don't use a lot today, but it means "face." Jesus' face was marred more than any man. Now that is one huge statement.

I remember when Mel Gibson's movie, *The Passion of the Christ* came out. Even though the depiction of Jesus' suffering was brutal, Mel Gibson said he had to tone it down. He admitted that it was worse than what was portrayed in the movie.[2]

If you remember the two men I mentioned earlier whose faces were disfigured by cancer, at least they looked human. I could tell they were men, despite the toll that disease had taken on them. Well, Jesus took on Himself all the sin, sickness, disease, and depravity of the world to such a degree that He no longer looked like a man. Jesus didn't just take sin in principle—a tiny taste of it—he took the full measure of every person's sin who has ever lived on this planet. It entered into His body. It entered into His soul. He felt all the shame, disgrace, and defilement that you and I have ever felt, multiplied billions of times over. He felt that in His soul, but His physical body was marred so that His face was worse than any other person's face that ever lived. Jesus was so marred that He didn't even look human.

God wasn't going to allow that to be put on His son to pay just *part* of the price! Jesus has already paid *everything* for you, praise God!

> Jesus...took the full measure of every person's sin who has ever lived on this planet.

The Nearly-Too-Good-to-Be-True News

For I am not ashamed of the gospel of Christ:
for it is the power of God unto salvation to
every one that believeth.

Romans 1:16

The meaning of the Greek word translated *salvation* here isn't limited only to the forgiveness of sins. It's also talking about healing, prosperity, and deliverance—everything Jesus came to do. Therefore, the power of God for you and me to receive salvation (forgiveness of sins, healing, prosperity, and deliverance) is released through the Gospel—the nearly-too-good-to-be-true news—of Jesus Christ.

The word *gospel* in the original Greek language is a word that was seldom used at the time the Bible was written. Practically nobody used the word, because it literally means "nearly-too-good-to-be-true news"—something so awesome it would be hard to believe. The nearly-too-good-to-be-true news of the Gospel is that you don't get what you deserve.

You get what Jesus deserves! Jesus bore your sin, rose from the grave, and overcame death and hell so you could have everything God has for you. That is nearly-too-good-to-be-true news, amen! When you think about it, that's the glory of the Gospel. We don't have to work and get God's love. We don't have to get to this place where we think, *Okay, now God can accept me.* He did it Himself!

> **You don't get what you deserve. You get what Jesus deserves!**

That's just the love of God! I love the Lord and He has been so good to me. He's treated me much better than I deserve. I've seen God just pour out His blessings, and it's better than anything I would have ever asked or thought (Eph. 3:20). I've had a lot of people say, "Well, you deserve it," and I've answered, "No, I don't deserve it." But I'm humble enough, and I'm going to receive it, praise God!

We don't deserve the blessings of God. First Corinthians 4:7 says, "*...what hast thou that thou didst not receive? Now if thou didst receive* it, *why dost* *thou glory, as if thou hadst not received* it." In other words, it's not as if you had produced those blessings based on your own goodness.

There are great things happening in my life and ministry, and I praise God for it all, but I guarantee you it's not because I deserve it. It's just because Jesus came and took all of God's judgment for my sin and my failure. Because of that, I get all of God's goodness. What a great deal!

What about Sin?

By now, you may be thinking, *This really is nearly-too-good-to-be-true news, but what about sins I may commit in the future?*

God has already placed all of our sin upon Jesus. He not only paid for all the sins of believers, but of unbelievers too. Christ paid for all the sins—past, present, and even future sins—of the entire world (1 John 2:2). All sins have been paid for!

God isn't angry. He's not judging us for our sin. Jesus drew all judgment to Himself at the cross. God is dealing with people today based on whether or not they've made Jesus their Lord.

Remember, people go to hell not because of their individual sins, but because they rejected Jesus. If you've accepted Christ, then you have a relationship with God. You're not going to do anything that will surprise the Lord, or that hasn't already been dealt with.

Every time you sin, you don't have to get it confessed and "back under the blood," or you're out of fellowship and relationship with God until you do so. Those things are being taught in many churches, but they're not what the Scripture reveals at all.

If we confess our sins, he is faithful and just to forgive us our sins, and to cleanse us from all unrighteousness.

1 John 1:9

This verse begs the questions: If forgiveness and cleansing are conditional on confessing our sins, then what happens if we don't confess our sins? Are they not forgiven? And if they aren't forgiven, then what are the consequences of that?

> **Every time you sin, you don't have to get it confessed and "back under the blood."**

The strictest interpretation of 1 John 1:9 would lead to the belief that if there is any unconfessed sin in our lives, we would not be forgiven. Although some have interpreted this verse to say just that, this certainly is not what this means.

The word *confess* simply means "to speak the same thing."[3] When we confess our sins, we are turning from our way of thinking and agreeing with the Lord that what we have done is wrong.

Our sin doesn't separate us from the Lord like it did under the Old Testament (Is. 59:1–2), and He no longer cuts us off like a cancer. All our sins have already been paid for. But as long as we walk in unconfessed sin, Satan has an inroad into our lives (Rom. 6:16). When we confess our sins, the forgiveness that is already a reality in our spirits becomes a reality in our soul and body. This cleanses us from all the attacks of the devil that we opened ourselves up to. Satan can work in the flesh of believers who have unconfessed sin. Satan cannot exist in the flesh of believers who have confessed their sins and understand and believe they are totally forgiven and cleansed from all unrighteousness (Rom. 5:21). So, the confession of sins encouraged here is not for our eternal salvation, or to maintain our relationship with God, but to rid us of the inroad Satan gains into our lives through our sins. Confessing that what we did was sin and repenting of that action closes a door on the devil and opens the door to the Lord.

The War Is Over

The sad fact is a lot of Christians don't know the war is over. We are still being told that God is imputing our sins unto us. They are still living like God is angry toward them.

I want to share a story that might illustrate this to you. In 1944, during World War II, Japanese Lt.

Hiroo Onoda[4] was sent to the island of Lubang in the Philippines. He was a part of the Japanese special forces trained in guerrilla warfare.

Lieutenant Onoda was ordered not to surrender or to kill himself under any circumstances. He was also told there would be propaganda sent by the Americans, but he was never to surrender.

At the end of the war, planes flew over the island with loudspeakers, proclaiming in Japanese that the fighting had ended. They dropped leaflets and did all kinds of things to spread the message, but Lieutenant Onoda thought that it was just propaganda, and he had been ordered not to surrender.

Because he was under the false impression that the war was still on, Lieutenant Onoda fought for nearly thirty more years. He continued engaging in guerrilla warfare on Lubang, killing several Filipinos in an effort to remain hidden. To survive, he ate coconuts and bananas during his entire time on the island.

There were actually four Japanese soldiers on the island. Two of them gave up and one died, but Lieutenant Onoda remained until his commander finally flew to the Philippines in the 1970s and gave him the order that the war was over, and he could surrender.

Because Lieutenant Onoda was still serving as a combatant, Filipino President Ferdinand Marcos pardoned him. He returned to Japan, where he was hailed as a hero.

For nearly thirty years after the end of World War II, this Japanese soldier was still fighting because he didn't realize the war was over.

Think about the hardships that he endured. Think about the separation from family and friends. Think about how he may have missed his culture and all of the things that he suffered that were completely unnecessary. Think about all the people who were hurt—and died—because he kept living as if a war was going on.

I'm saying to you that there are Christians who are suffering, not understanding that the war is over. You are being told that God is still holding your sins against you. You are being told that if you have any sin in your life, God is not going to bless you. You are being told that God will not answer your prayer, that God is angry at you, and that God is upset at you.

How long will you keep living as if the war is still on and miss out on all God has for you? I encourage you to accept all that Jesus has done for us, and celebrate with the angels that there is *"on earth peace, good will toward men."*

Missing the Parade

And you, being dead in your sins and the uncircumcision of your flesh, hath he quickened together with him, having forgiven you all trespasses; blotting out the handwriting of ordinances that was against us, which was contrary to us, and took it out of the way, nailing it to his cross; and *having spoiled principalities and powers, he made a shew of them openly, triumphing over them in it.*

Colossians 2:13–15

Jesus not only conquered Satan and his forces, but He spoiled them. He stripped them of all their power and authority. He also made an exhibit of them. That's what the Greek word *deigmatizó*, which was translated *"made a shew,"* means.[5]

> **How long will you keep living as if the war is still on and miss out on all God has for you?**

The phrase *triumphing over* came from the Greek word *thriambeuo*, and it means "to make an acclamatory procession, i.e. (figuratively) to conquer or (by Hebraism) to give victory."[6] This Greek word was from a base that described what the Romans called "a triumphal procession."[7]

The Romans would take a conquered king or general and strip him naked, tie him to a horse or chariot, cut off his big toes and thumbs, and have a victory parade. This was to show all the Roman citizens that the one who had been a threat would never cause them any more trouble. If this man had any power, he would never allow such a parade. But he couldn't hold a sword anymore or do anything but hobble.

This is what God did with the devil. He totally spoiled him, and Satan is void of any power or authority to oppress us anymore. But the problem is that much of the body of Christ has missed the parade. They don't know Satan has been defeated. Sadly, many churches are the agent of Satan's intimidation through their wrong teachings on his authority. We must show them this parade through the pages of Scripture so they will not live in fear of a defeated foe.

Conclusion

Most of us believe that God moves in our life only when we're worthy. We've tied His ability to our goodness. The moment you do that, Satan will defeat you because your own heart will condemn you and let you know that you don't deserve it. But that's not the message Jesus brought. He wasn't imputing man's sins unto him. He told us to preach a message that tells people, "The war is over. God isn't mad anymore!"

Now, this doesn't mean that it's all up to God. If it were, then you would receive because God is a good God. He has nothing but good things in store for you. However, you must believe to receive. You don't have to be holy and do everything just right, but you do have to believe. If you feel so unworthy and think that you've messed up so badly that God doesn't love you, that's unbelief. That is not the message of the Gospel, and it's the very thing that's keeping your faith from working.

Faith works by love (Gal. 5:6). If you understood how much God loved you—that He carries your picture around in His wallet, that He isn't angry, disappointed, or ashamed of you, and that He's proud

> **You don't have to be holy and do everything just right, but you do have to believe.**

of you—your faith would go through the roof. You'd say, "Any God who could love me and overlook all the stupid things I've done is an awesome God. If He'll do that, He'll do anything!"

Now then we are ambassadors for Christ, as though God did beseech you by us: we pray you in Christ's stead, be ye reconciled to God.

2 Corinthians 5:20

That's my purpose in writing this booklet. I want to help you become reconciled to God. God has reconciled Himself to you. He has forgiven your sins and taken them away. He's not angry with you. God is now friendly and harmonized with you. Will you reconcile yourself to God? Will you now accept what He has said?

This is the message Christians are supposed to be sharing—that the war is over!

Further Study

If you enjoyed this booklet and would like to learn more about some of the things I've shared, I suggest these teachings:

- *The War Is Over* (full-length book, study guide, DVD, CD or USB format
- *The Word Made Flesh*
- *Spirit, Soul & Body*
- *Eternal Life*

These teachings are available free of charge at **awmi.net/video** or for purchase in book, study guide, CD, DVD, or USB formats at **awmi.net/store**.

Receive Jesus as Your Savior

Choosing to receive Jesus Christ as your Lord and Savior is the most important decision you'll ever make!

God's Word promises, *"That if thou shalt confess with thy mouth the Lord Jesus, and shalt believe in thine heart that God hath raised him from the dead, thou shalt be saved. For with the heart man believeth unto righteousness; and with the mouth confession is made unto salvation"* (Rom. 10:9–10). *"For whosoever shall call upon the name of the Lord shall be saved"* (Rom. 10:13). By His grace, God has already done everything to provide salvation. Your part is simply to believe and receive.

Pray out loud: "Jesus, I confess that You are my Lord and Savior. I believe in my heart that God raised You from the dead. By faith in Your Word, I receive salvation now. Thank You for saving me."

The very moment you commit your life to Jesus Christ, the truth of His Word instantly comes to pass in your spirit. Now that you're born again, there's a brand-new you!

Please contact us and let us know that you've prayed to receive Jesus as your Savior. We'd like to send you some free materials to help you on your new journey. Call our Helpline: **719-635-1111** (available 24 hours a day, seven days a week) to speak to a staff member who is here to help you understand and grow in your new relationship with the Lord.

Welcome to your new life!

Receive the Holy Spirit

As His child, your loving heavenly Father wants to give you the supernatural power you need to live a new life. *"For every one that asketh receiveth; and he that seeketh findeth; and to him that knocketh it shall be opened...how much more shall* your *heavenly Father give the Holy Spirit to them that ask him?"* (Luke 11:10–13).

All you have to do is ask, believe, and receive!

Pray this: "Father, I recognize my need for Your power to live a new life. Please fill me with Your Holy Spirit. By faith, I receive it right now. Thank You for baptizing me. Holy Spirit, You are welcome in my life."

Some syllables from a language you don't recognize will rise up from your heart to your mouth

(1 Cor. 14:14). As you speak them out loud by faith, you're releasing God's power from within and building yourself up in the spirit (1 Cor. 14:4). You can do this whenever and wherever you like.

It doesn't really matter whether you felt anything or not when you prayed to receive the Lord and His Spirit. If you believed in your heart that you received, then God's Word promises you did. *"Therefore I say unto you, What things soever ye desire, when ye pray, believe that ye receive them, and ye shall have them"* (Mark 11:24). God always honors His Word—believe it!

We would like to rejoice with you and help you understand more fully what has taken place in your life!

Please contact us to let us know that you've prayed to be filled with the Holy Spirit and to request the book *The New You & the Holy Spirit*. This book will explain in more detail about the benefits of being filled with the Holy Spirit and speaking in tongues. Call our Helpline: **719-635-1111** (available 24 hours a day, seven days a week).

Call for Prayer

If you need prayer for any reason, you can call our Helpline, 24 hours a day, seven days a week at **719-635-1111**. A trained prayer minister will answer your call and pray with you.

Every day, we receive testimonies of healings and other miracles from our Helpline, and we are ministering God's nearly-too-good-to-be-true message of the Gospel to more people than ever. So, I encourage you to call today!

About the Author

Andrew Wommack's life was forever changed the moment he encountered the supernatural love of God on March 23, 1968. As a renowned Bible teacher and author, Andrew has made it his mission to change the way the world sees God.

Andrew's vision is to go as far and deep with the Gospel as possible. His message goes far through the *Gospel Truth* television program, which is available to over half the world's population. The message goes deep through discipleship at Charis Bible College, headquartered in Woodland Park, Colorado. Founded in 1994, Charis has campuses across the United States and around the globe.

Andrew also has an extensive library of teaching materials in print, audio, and video. More than 200,000 hours of free teachings can be accessed at **awmi.net**.

Endnotes

1.   Winston Churchill, "Sinews of Peace (Iron Curtain Speech)," Westminster College, Fulton, MO, March 5, 1946, accessed March 3, 2023, https://www.nationalchurchillmuseum.org/sinews-of-peace-iron-curtain-speech.html.

2.   *The Passion of the Christ* (Movie Review), *PluggedIn*, Focus on the Family, Accessed March 3, 2023, https://www.pluggedin.com/movie-reviews/passionofthechrist/.

3.   *Vine's Expository Dictionary of New Testament Words*, s.v. "confess," accessed March 3, 2023, https://www.blueletterbible.org/search/Dictionary/viewTopic.cfm?topic=VT0000537.

4.   Robert D. McFadden, "Hiroo Onoda, Soldier Who Hid in Jungle for Decades, Dies at 91," *New York Times*, January 17, 2014, accessed March 3, 2023, https://www.nytimes.com/2014/01/18/world/asia/hiroo-onoda-imperial-japanese-army-officer-dies-at-91.html.

5. *Strong's Exhaustive Concordance of the Bible*, "G1165, deigmatizó," accessed March 3, 2023, https://www.bibletools.org/index.cfm/fuseaction/Lexicon.show/ID/G1165/deigmatizo.htm.

6. *Strong's Exhaustive Concordance of the Bible*, "2358: thriambeuo," accessed March 3, 2023, https://www.bibletools.org/index.cfm/fuseaction/Lexicon.show/ID/G2358/thriambeuo.htm.

7. *Robertson's Word Pictures*, "Colossians 2," accessed March 3, 2023, https://www.studylight.org/commentaries/eng/rwp/colossians-2.html.

Contact Information

Andrew Wommack Ministries, Inc.
PO Box 3333
Colorado Springs, CO 80934-3333
info@awmi.net
awmi.net

Helpline: 719-635-1111 (available 24/7)

Charis Bible College
info@charisbiblecollege.org
844-360-9577
CharisBibleCollege.org

For a complete list of our offices, visit
awmi.net/contact-us.

Connect with us on social media.

Andrew's LIVING COMMENTARY BIBLE SOFTWARE

Andrew Wommack's *Living Commentary* Bible study software is a user-friendly, downloadable program. It's like reading the Bible with Andrew at your side, sharing his revelation with you verse by verse.

Main features:

- Bible study software with a grace-and-faith perspective
- Over 26,000 notes by Andrew on verses from Genesis through Revelation
- *Matthew Henry's Concise Commentary*
- 11 Bible versions
- 2 concordances: *Englishman's Concordance* and *Strong's Concordance*
- 2 dictionaries: *Collaborative International Dictionary* and *Holman's Dictionary*
- Atlas with biblical maps
- Bible and *Living Commentary* statistics
- Quick navigation, including history of verses
- Robust search capabilities (for the Bible and Andrew's notes)
- "Living" (i.e., constantly updated and expanding)
- Ability to create personal notes

Whether you're new to studying the Bible or a seasoned Bible scholar, you'll gain a deeper revelation of the Word from a grace-and-faith perspective.

Purchase Andrew's *Living Commentary* today at **awmi.net/living**, and grow in the Word with Andrew.

Item code: 8350

ANDREW WOMMACK MINISTRIES

Your peace doesn't have to ebb and flow with the tides of circumstance. Build your life on the solid foundation of the Word.

Visit our website for teachings, videos, testimonies, and other resources that will encourage you with truth for any situation and help you learn God's plan for relationships, finances, faith, and more.

"I was lost deep in the world. . . . I started seeking the truth, and through AWM's resources, I have been set free . . . including receiving miracles of finances when everything seemed impossible. I am at peace with myself. I thank AWM for sharing the truth, which has freed me to understand God."

— David M.

Be empowered to live the victorious life God intended for you! Visit **awmi.net** to access our library of free resources.

Teaching God's unconditional love and grace.

CHARIS
BIBLE COLLEGE

God has more for you.

Are you longing to find your God-given purpose? At Charis Bible College you will establish a firm foundation in the Word of God and receive hands-on ministry experience to **find, follow,** and **fulfill** your purpose.

Scan the QR code for a free Charis teaching!

CharisBibleCollege.org
Admissions@awmcharis.com
(844) 360-9577

Change your life. **Change the world.**